At the Vanguard

AT THE
VANGUARD

MAKING AND SAVING HISTORY AT HISTORICALLY
BLACK COLLEGES AND UNIVERSITIES

NATIONAL MUSEUM
of AFRICAN AMERICAN
HISTORY & CULTURE

g

National Museum of African American History and Culture
Smithsonian Institution, Washington, D.C., in association with D Giles Limited

Published on the occasion of *At the Vanguard: Making and Saving History at Historically Black Colleges and Universities*, an exhibition created by the National Museum of African American History and Culture in collaboration with the Smithsonian Institution Traveling Exhibition Service.

For the National Museum of African American History and Culture
Series Editor: Tulani Salahu-Din
Volume Co-Editor: Marion McGee
Publications Coordinator: Douglas Remley

For D Giles Limited
Copyedited and proofread by Jodi Simpson
Designed by Alfonso Iacurci
Produced by GILES, an imprint of D Giles Limited
Bound and printed in Italy

First published in 2025 by GILES
An imprint of D Giles Limited
66 High Street
Lewes
BN7 1XG
www.gilesltd.com

EU GPSR Authorised Representative
LOGOS EUROPE, 9 rue Nicolas Poussin, 17000, LA ROCHELLE, France
E-mail: Contact@logoseurope.eu

ISBN: 978-1-917273-07-7

This project is supported by:

NATIONAL ENDOWMENT FOR THE
HUMANITIES

BANK OF AMERICA

Southern Company Foundation

TJX

With additional support from: CBRE

MIX
Paper | Supporting responsible forestry
FSC® C015829

CONTENTS

FOREWORD

Tulani Salahu-Din and Marion McGee
Co-editors

Historically Black Colleges and Universities (HBCUs) stand as pillars of academic excellence, artistic expression, and collective activism. These institutions were pioneers in creating systems for collecting and preserving the art, historical objects, and cultural ephemera produced through the lived experiences of African Americans. Established by visionaries who believed in the transformative power of education, the archives and museums on these campuses persist as enduring symbols of resilience and fortitude.

The National Museum of African American History and Culture (NMAAHC) demonstrates its commitment to advancing the preservation efforts of HBCUs by digitizing and exhibiting their collections to honor and elevate the legacies of these historic institutions. Through the History and Culture Access Consortium, the Museum ensures the stories–embedded in the artifacts, archives, and cultural treasures of these HBCUs–are conserved and shared, creating a bridge between their vivid pasts and dynamic futures.

The NMAAHC's efforts to advance the digitization and visibility of collections from its five HBCU partners are a testament to the enduring significance of these institutions in the fabric of American history. These HBCU collections are essential to understanding and appreciating the African American experience.

The *At the Vanguard* exhibition and this companion publication are the fulfillment of a promise to be intentional about our collaborative work with our HBCU colleagues to ensure that their institutional collections are amplified and digitally accessible far beyond geographic borders. This book is a small sampling of the many compelling objects, images, and stories found in the exhibition. *At the Vanguard* underscores the richness of HBCU art and archival collections while sharing our organization's mission to promote the study and appreciation of African American life, art, history, and culture.

Art Exhibition Opening,
March 20, 1958 (detail)

THE HISTORY AND CULTURE ACCESS CONSORTIUM
PARTNERING WITH HBCUS

Marion McGee and Auntaneshia Staveloz
Office of Strategic Partnerships, NMAAHC

The History and Culture Access Consortium (HCAC) is a first-of-its-kind initiative designed to create lasting benefits for museums and archives at Historically Black Colleges and Universities (HBCUs). By preserving their cultural legacy and enhancing resource availability, the HCAC makes known the under-told history of African Americans and their essential role in the story of America. The initiative is organized by the Office of Strategic Partnerships (OSP) at the National Museum of African American History and Culture (NMAAHC), which was established as part of the legislation creating the NMAAHC in 2003. The OSP strengthens the sustainability of historical, cultural, and art institutions.

Within the arts and culture sectors, OSP serves as a resource for partnership and professional development. OSP established the HCAC following a decade-long effort to deliver on the Museum's legislative mandate to work intentionally with our HBCU colleagues to sustain the existence and legacy of our collective institutions. In 2012 and 2013, OSP engaged with HBCUs through a series of listening sessions, topically focused questionnaires, a national survey, and professional convenings to understand the collective needs of their museums and archives. Beginning in 2014, OSP sponsored over fifty undergraduate interns to work and learn in HBCU museums and galleries nationwide.

In 2018, the NMAAHC welcomed presidents and cultural leaders from ten HBCUs to a landmark HBCU Leadership Summit, the first of its kind for the Smithsonian Institution. The summit brought together top administrators

HCAC Senior Leadership Meeting, Jackson, Mississippi, 2022

HCAC intern Christopher Jackson photographing artwork at Clark Atlanta University, 2023

to explore issues facing academic museums and repositories, to investigate strategic solutions, and to identify sustainable efforts to support these historic institutions. The information gathered from the 2018 Leadership Summit, in combination with the data generated from formal research evaluations, led to ongoing collaboration and strategic conversations to explicitly define the kind of investments needed to address the short- and long-term needs of HBCU cultural institutions.

This work culminated in the establishment of the HBCU History and Culture Access Consortium, launched in 2021, with five inaugural partners representing museums and archives from Clark Atlanta, Florida A&M, Jackson State, Texas Southern, and Tuskegee Universities. The initiative uses a systems approach to prioritize directives that strengthen university leaders' support of their museums and archives and encourage collaboration among HBCU repositories. Together, these efforts create a model for increased visibility of collections and archival materials in a meaningful way through digital access and collections sharing among participating institutions.

The initiative is comprised of five core components: 1) Technical Training and Leadership Development; 2) Talent Pipeline Development; 3) Collections Care and Digitization; 4) Traveling Exhibition and Exhibition Publication; and 5) Project Evaluation and Expansion. The initiative centers the importance of building a community of practice that provides a safe and supportive forum for listening, planning, and implementing strategies that address the staff capacity, technological integration, and organizational funding needs of institutional repositories of Black art, history, and culture.

The HCAC demonstrates an unwavering commitment to the cultural institutions, archives, and museums through our collective efforts to impact, empower, and sustain the preservation of African American art, history, and culture on Historically Black College and University campuses for generations to come.

HISTORIC HBCU COLLECTIONS

HOW WE REMEMBER WHAT MANY FORGET

Tulani Salahu-Din
Museum Specialist, Language and Literature,
Office of Curatorial Affairs, NMAAHC

Phillis Wheatley, 1973 (detail), Elizabeth Catlett

"Black memory workers at HBCUs across the nation have preserved and provided access to collections."

—Holly A. Smith, archivist, Spelman College, 2024

Museums, libraries, and archives help to preserve the cultural heritage of a people, of a nation. On the campuses of Historically Black Colleges and Universities (HBCUs), these repositories represent stellar efforts to collect, preserve, and share the complex cultural heritage of African Americans. As varied sources of memory for future generations, they also house collections that document their own institutional histories and the experiences of other African Diasporic communities. These rare collections speak loudly from quiet spaces, in archival boxes and storage bins, on hallway walls and moveable racks, telling inspiring stories of creativity, genius, and resistance and reminding the nation of truths that would otherwise be forgotten.

Through the revolutionary work of archivists—like Dorothy Porter and her pioneering achievement in cataloguing at Howard University—and other committed memory workers, the collections reveal an intellectual and physical abundance of African American material culture. Since 1868, when Hampton University founded a museum on its campus, these living, breathing repositories have been harbingers of sacred truth telling.

Fundamentally, they help preserve invaluable aspects of United States history that, without their existence, would be shamefully lost to the nation.

Featured in this volume are images of objects and archival materials surveyed in the campus collections of the Museum's five HBCU partners. The purpose of presenting these materials is to offer readers a compelling glimpse into the transformative and revolutionary world of HBCUs—into their vibrant and varied campus culture and rigorous, life-altering academic programs—and to uncover the complex stories that the objects and archival materials in their collections tell us.

Selecting the images of objects and archival materials for this publication began with mining the varied collections of the five partner HBCUs. Holdings at the Margaret Walker Center at Jackson State University trumpet local community histories and civil rights and Black Panther activism. They boast photography by community activist and JSU photographer Doris Derby and the prized Margaret Walker papers, encompassing in part her personal journals and letters to Walker from other prominent writers, including Richard Wright and Alice Walker. In contrast, the University Museum at Texas Southern University is an authority on African

Jackson State University archivist Angela Stewart working in the Margaret Walker Archives, 2019

American art and art of the African Diaspora. Its collection stewards engaging works by both faculty and student artists, some thoroughly trained by the renowned Texas Southern art educator Dr. John Biggers.

Regarded as one of the largest archives of African American materials, the Meek-Eaton Black Archives Research Center and Museum at Florida A&M University cradles thousands of artifacts and an even greater number of archival records related to a range of subjects, such as dance, music, drama, and civil rights. Further, the Clark Atlanta University Art Museum features a premiere collection of African American art from collectors, estates, and foundations. The museum welcomes visitors to view its acclaimed *Art of the Negro* wall murals, created by the legendary artist and teacher Hale Woodruff between 1950 and 1951. Conveying a profound sense of placemaking for art, the murals remain accessible in the foyer just outside the museum's doors. Lastly, significant holdings at the Tuskegee University Archives range from fiscal and administrative records documenting institutional history and one of the largest collections in the United States documenting the lynching of African Americans. Additional holdings include materials on the founder Booker T. Washington and prominent faculty, such as scientist George Washington Carver, data collector Monroe Work, and career photographers C. M. Battey and P. H. Polk.

Like the themes explored in the traveling exhibition of the same name, the revealing and sometimes riveting stories in this companion publication use objects from these five collections to attest to the aesthetic value of African American cultural production on university campuses, the persistent development and expansion of HBCU academic programs, and the dynamics of student-led activism on campuses and throughout surrounding communities. Organized into four main sections, beginning with "The Revolutionary and Transformative World of HBCUs" and followed by three thematic sections focusing on the arts, academics, and activism, this remarkable assembly of images will hopefully inspire readers to engage with, reflect on, and possibly examine further the unforgettable stories they represent.

The Boss, 1932
P. H. Polk

Constance Slaughter-Harvey during hearings of the President's Commission on Campus Unrest, Jackson, Mississippi, 1970
Doris Derby

NO LESS LOVELY BEING DARK

In 1926, the poem "From the Dark Tower"—by Harlem Renaissance poet Countee Cullen—appeared in the avant-garde publication *Fire!! Devoted to Younger Negro Artists*. An excerpt from the poem reads, "The night whose sable breast relieves the stark, / White stars is no less lovely being dark, / And there are buds that cannot bloom at all / In light, but crumple, piteous, and fall." The beauty of the night sky stands as a metaphor for the "loveliness" of the darker people and the aesthetic value of their cultural arts. This section features images representing the beauty of African American cultural output—the literary, visual, and performing arts.

One vivid example of the beauty to which Cullen alludes lies in two images of women pulled from the archives at Tuskegee and Jackson State that capture the women's serious countenance as they pursue their earnest goals. The 1932 photograph titled *The Boss* shows an unnamed, formerly enslaved woman standing in self-command, gazing directly into the camera (p. 14). P. H. Polk (1898-1984), who served as Tuskegee University's official photographer from the 1930s to 1970s, met the woman while she was setting up her produce stand in Macon County, Alabama, and asked to photograph her. Through this image and others, Polk gained a reputation for his work in portraiture, and today, much of his photography resides in the Tuskegee archives.

Similarly, decades later in 1970, Doris Derby (1939-2022), a staff photographer at Jackson State University, photographed a young civil rights lawyer, Constance Slaughter-Harvey, who represented the families of two students killed by police at Jackson State (p. 15). Taken in Jackson, Mississippi, during a hearing of the President's Commission on Campus Unrest, Derby's photograph shows Slaughter-Harvey seated at a microphone, her eyes cut to the side in view of her audience, her lips parted as if preparing to speak. Known for her focus on children and women of the Civil Rights Movement, Derby elevated the visibility of lesser-known women of the movement. Her work lives in the Margaret Walker Center at Jackson State. Polk and Derby collectively amassed a visual record that documents the cultural aesthetics and momentum of their times.

In addition to photography, music and performing arts have flourished at HBCUs, and evidence of these cultural expressions dwells within their collections. HBCUs have served as training grounds for music and performance professionals and hubs of musical and theatrical expression for all who appreciate the sounds and visuals of great performances. Through their collections, HBCU museums and archives have documented the emotive and intellectual power of song, instrumentality, and the performing arts as part of the distinct artistic legacy of their institutions.

A compelling part of this legacy is the cultural phenomenon of the high-spirited marching bands that display their talents at sporting events and, most famously, at homecoming games. Between 1946 and 1998, Dr. William P. Foster (1919–2010), whose image is captured in photographs at the Meek-Eaton archives, emerged as one of the world's most renowned band directors. As the creator and director of Florida A&M University's Marching "100," he brought laudable recognition to the State of Florida. Recognized also throughout the country, the Marching "100" has entertained thousands and revolutionized marching-band techniques. As an artist, educator, and band leader, Foster cultivated his own unique style of band pageantry and fashioned a new dimension of the art form.

A MIND IS A MARVELOUS THING

Originally established as normal schools, seminaries, and institutes, with only a few buildings on their grounds, HBCUs would grow and develop into institutions with a full range of academic programs. To address the growing intellectual and social needs of students and scholars, and the communities they served, HBCUs broadened the scope of their institutional goals and diversified academic offerings, creating life-changing and life-sustaining schools of medicine, dentistry, law, education, and engineering, generally in the face of disturbing inequities in funding. Faculty at these institutions engaged in rigorous intellectual work, conducting groundbreaking research and making important contributions to fields such as business, education, the social sciences, and global studies. Students and communities nationwide and abroad have been the explicit focus or beneficiaries of their research.

One shining example of this invigorating research is the vital data collecting of Monroe and Florence Work at Tuskegee University. From 1908 to 1938, Monroe Work (1866–1945) served as the director of Tuskegee Institute's Department of Records and Research, where he and his wife Florence (1877–1955) compiled data on the condition and lives of African Americans and published their data in an encyclopedia titled the *Negro Year Book*. The Tuskegee University Archives yield access to a complete collection of these essential resources. The Works helped to ensure that crucial knowledge about African Americans would not go unrecorded and would prove useful in revealing social setbacks as well as milestones in social progress.

Jackson State University educator Dr. Jane Ellen McAllister (1899–1996) also understood the educational and cultural value of compiling and retaining historical records. Long before she became the first African American woman to earn a doctorate in education from the Teachers College at Columbia University, McAllister was a student at Talladega College, the oldest private HBCU in Alabama, and a meticulous record keeper of her school expenses. In her personal archive are expense sheets on which she recorded the monthly costs of attending Talladega. In March 1917 her expenses were two dollars and fifty cents for tuition, eleven dollars for board, and thirty cents for books and stationery. This attention to detail and the value she placed on retaining records characterized her work

as a seasoned researcher and leader in teacher education training at Jackson State from 1952 to 1967. McAllister joined the faculty twelve years after the school emerged as a four-year teachers' college. The Jackson State historical marker, housed at the Margaret Walker Center, shows that in 1940 the school "became a state teachers college for Negroes." (p. 33) McAllister would also enhance teacher education programs at numerous other HBCUs, including Virginia State, Southern, Fisk, Grambling State, and Miner Teachers College, now the University of the District of Columbia, to which she devoted twenty-five years of her career.

DOING BATTLE WHERE WE STAND

Beginning in the early twentieth century, HBCU students ignited activism that helped bring about radical change to their schools, local and regional communities, and the nation. Their roles in high-profile liberation struggles catalyzed the Civil Rights Movement, gave birth to the Black Power Movement, and have continued to help usher in social reform. HBCU students have held their colleges, state governments, and the country to the highest

Jane Ellen McAllister's Talladega College expense sheet, March 1917

Folio........ *Ellen McAllister*

To TALLADEGA COLLEGE, Dr.

Expenses For The Month Of *March* 1917

Balance.			
To Incidental Fee,			
(charged on entrance)			
To Board,	11		
" Tuition,	2	50	
" Music,	5	00	
" Washing,			
" Laundry articles,			
" Meals carried to room,			
" Breakages,		10	
" Books and stationery,		30	
"	18	90	
"			
By Deposit,			
" Labor during month,	3	42	
Balance,	15	48	

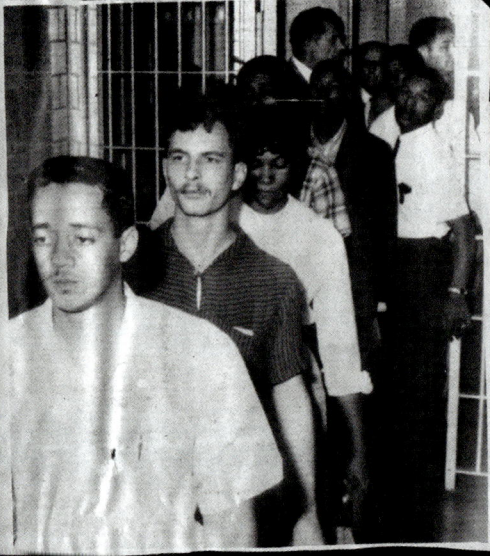

PHOTO EDITORIAL FORWARD TIMES,

Time For A Bit Of Soul Searching

This week 27 of our young college students walked into the county jail and surrendered themselves. They were mugged, finger printed and locked up.

The immediate impact upon the community ranged from extreme concern - rallys to raise funds, letters to the governor, telegrams to the president and open expressions about the shame of it all - to complete indifference by a wide segment of our population who were just plain too busy enjoying their new won freedoms to bother about stopping long enough to lend a hand or a coin.

Aid came from some extremes also. Early Tuesday morning a white professor from the University of Houston walked into our office and made a cash donation after stating that he wished that he could do more.

About mid-day, a Negro laborer in faded coveralls and muddy shoes walked into our office and gave to us all of the money that he had in his pocket.

He said "This is all that I have but I think those young people down there in jail need to be out."

Tuesday evening a volunteer worker walked along the row of lunch counter seats at Grant's and solicited funds from the several Negroes seated there enjoying their food. A few understood and gave. Far too many looked at the worker like they thought she was crazy. They didn't know that except for the students locked up in the county jail, they would have had to stand and get their lunch handed to them out of a window.

The students all lost time from their classes and many were not able to take their final examinations. All now have their names permanently placed upon the police files.

People who sacrifice for the good of his fellowman expect to be ignored and forgotten. They do the things that they do because they believe them to be right. They are not looking for praise.

But can we who enjoy the new freedoms afford not to praise them?

Can we afford not to help those who have helped us so much?

Can we afford to forget them?

Search your souls. If you haven't made a move to help these young freedom fighters locked up in jail to get free, how can you live with yourself?

Page from John W. Bland's scrapbook documenting the Progressive Youth Association's Houston Sit-in Movement, 1960

"Search your souls. If you haven't made a move to help these young freedom fighters locked up in jail to get free, how can you live with yourself?"

—Varee Shields Jr., *Houston Forward Times*, May 19, 1962

standards of excellence and equality. The records of these battles reside in HBCU archives–in student newspapers, yearbooks, alumni scrapbooks, and photograph albums.

When John Willie Bland of Houston, Texas, sat down to neatly place news clippings into a black leather scrapbook, he was thinking about the significance of historical records in maintaining collective memory of

the Houston student sit-ins. Only two years had passed since his 1958 high school graduation and entrance into Texas Southern University as a business major. Upon hearing about the sit-ins at the Woolworth's lunch counter in Greensboro in February 1960, he helped mobilize students to join him in founding the Progressive Youth Association (PYA) and staging Houston's first sit-in on March 4,

1960, at the local Weingarten's grocery store. Titled "The Progressive Youth Association: Houston Sit-In Movement," Bland's scrapbook would find its way into the Special Collections at Texas Southern, where it resides in digital format for all to see. The contents of the scrapbook tell the story of peaceful student protests, arrests, and lockups, and of the efforts of local citizens to raise money for the students' release. The sit-ins and arrests garnered national attention, and Freedom Riders arrived in Houston in support of the student protests. A series of sit-ins would follow with Bland as the spokesperson for the PYA, and by August 1960, most Houston lunch counters were desegregated. Hotels, department stores, and restaurants followed suit. The student-led protests represent watershed moments in Houston's civil rights history and a longstanding tradition of radical student action emanating from HBCUs, which remain an essential source of unmitigated optimism in the ongoing struggle for equal rights for all people of the United States.

At the Vanguard draws attention to the representation of the African American past as revealed through multifarious collections on the campuses of Clark Atlanta, Florida A&M, Jackson State, Tuskegee, and Texas Southern Universities. Through the genius and commitment of memory workers who develop, preserve, and share these collections, the nation—as heirs and beneficiaries of the knowledge the collections generate—can always remember integral and foundational aspects of its history that would otherwise be forgotten. The rare and evocative images presented in this book help readers to assimilate that history and understand how it has shaped and continues to shape the present moment. This understanding can only enrich the nation and empower people in their pursuit of information and awareness, and in their ongoing struggle for a more just society and world.

Florida A&M Marching "100"
performing during the Louis Vuitton
Men's Fashion Show at the Louvre in
Paris, France, June 2022 (detail)
Tony Leavell

HIGHLIGHTS FROM THE COLLECTIONS

THE REVOLUTIONARY AND TRANSFORMATIVE WORLD OF HBCUS

Historically Black Colleges and Universities (HBCUs) are revolutionary and transformative. In 1837, the founding of Cheyney University of Pennsylvania, the first institution of higher learning for "Colored" youth, set in motion a revolution in higher education. HBCUs established after Cheyney would in time become major citadels of learning and remarkably vibrant cultural sites for those legally denied a formal education. HBCUs immersed students in self-empowering educational experiences that they could not access anywhere else. In doing so, they immeasurably transformed the lives of enslaved, formerly enslaved, and free individuals as well as generations of their descendants—an unprecedented educational phenomenon in world history.

During slavery, underground schools in various states comprised a vast system of education that enslaved communities developed to gain the knowledge and skills denied them. In Georgia, for example, adults and children secretly attended schools in the homes of educated members within their communities. HBCUs, known then and after slavery as institutes, industrial and training schools, or seminaries, were an outgrowth of racial discrimination in education. Through their

sheer endurance, they have remained a formidable force against inequity in higher education.

As the needs of their communities grew, so too did HBCUs and their approaches to education. Into the late nineteenth and early twentieth centuries, they began diversifying and expanding their academic offerings, establishing schools of medicine, dentistry, law, engineering, and education. Departments dedicated to the arts nurtured creatives and provided platforms to showcase their works. HBCU campuses, part of the lifeblood of African American communities, became enlivened gathering spaces with inspirational choirs, foot-stomping step shows, and riveting theatrical performances. Crowds cheered at homecoming games featuring high-stepping marching bands, and students assembled to hear the fiery speeches of activists, recitations of poets, and formal debates of other students. In both the arts and sciences, HBCUs would emerge as the primary producers of African American professionals while representing only 3 percent of the nation's four-year colleges.

Equally as revolutionary and transformative were the collecting and archiving practices on HBCU campuses, beginning as early as 1868. HBCUs took

Jackson State University Undergraduate Commencement, 2018

the lead in preserving African American material culture and institutional history, including their groundbreaking scientific research, oral histories of formerly enslaved community members, and the successful engagement of students in social activism. While mainstream American museums and archives disregarded and devalued African American materials, HBCU archivists, curators, and librarians collected, preserved, and exhibited these treasures, asserting their value as integral to American identity.

Today, 60 percent of HBCUs have an archive, gallery, or museum founded by pioneers in preserving materials reflective of the history and culture of their schools, African American communities, and people of the African Diaspora. Despite historical obstacles, these collections reveal the power of generations of intellectual and creative excellence. Through a shared sense of mission and vision, HBCUs and their repositories reflect an enduring belief in the transformative value of education. They also exhibit a sustained commitment to enriching the landscape of higher education and, most fundamentally, the individual lives of their students.

Tulani Salahu-Din
Museum Specialist, Language and Literature, Office of Curatorial Affairs, NMAAHC

Tuskegee University

Tuskegee University was founded in 1881 in a one-room building as the Negro Normal School in Tuskegee by George Campbell, a former enslaver, and Lewis Adams, a formerly enslaved person, tinsmith, and community leader. The school rose to national prominence under Dr. Booker T. Washington, who led the institution from 1881 to 1915 and helped secure its independence from the State of Alabama as the renamed Tuskegee Normal and Industrial Institute in 1892.

Arithmetic Class,
A Problem in Brick
Masonry, 1906
Frances Benjamin
Johnston

Bricks made by students at Tuskegee Institute, late 19th– early 20th century

–

Many Tuskegee University students worked on campus in lieu of paying for tuition. Students would participate in brick-laying, welding, and woodworking around campus. Learning through vocational training was an approach that allowed students to acquire expertise in construc-tion trades and promoted economic self-sufficiency. By building the campus brick by brick, students literally and figuratively shaped its develop-ment. Several of the buildings that still stand today were built by students in the late nineteenth century.

Clark Atlanta University

Clark Atlanta University was formed in 1988 with the consolidation of Atlanta University and Clark College. Founded in 1865 by the American Missionary Association, Atlanta University was the nation's first institution to award graduate degrees to African Americans. Clark College, established four years later in 1869, was the nation's first four-year liberal arts college to serve a primarily African American student population.

Art Exhibition Opening,
March 20, 1958

The Yellow Bird, 1951
Hale Woodruff
–

As the founding faculty
member of the Atlanta
University art depart-
ment, renowned
painter and printmaker
Hale Aspacio Woodruff
helped make the
university an impor-
tant Southern hub for
training and exhibiting
Black artists during the
mid-twentieth century.
His advice to young
artists: "Create a unity
out of art and the
facts of life."

Texas Southern University

Although initially established to educate African Americans, Texas Southern University graduates students from a broad range of cultural backgrounds. The university and its affiliated law school were established by the state legislature as Texas State University for Negroes in 1947–to avoid having to desegregate the all-white University of Texas. The Houston College for Negroes (formerly Houston Colored Junior College) merged with the new university to provide the necessary administrative structure and temporary facilities. Over successive decades, a new expansive campus was built, departments were added, and new programs were launched to house the growing institution.

Untitled (terra cotta head), 1970
Johnny Jones
–

After its 1949 establishment, TSU recruited faculty artists from around the country to teach visual arts, theater, music, and dance. This faculty, which included visual artists John Biggers and Carroll Simms, helped develop TSU into a thriving midcentury center for the cultural arts of African Americans and the larger African Diaspora. Through painting and sculpting, both educators encouraged students to embrace Afrocentric styles.

TSU art student Curtis Watson at work, 1970s
John Biggers

Jackson State University

Jackson State University was founded in 1877 in Natchez, Mississippi, as the Natchez Seminary by the American Baptist Home Mission Society. The school moved to Jackson in 1892. Expansion of its curriculum and building programs was accompanied by several name changes. Today, JSU's mission is to provide quality teaching, research, and services to its students and communities.

Students outside Ayer Hall, 2016

–

Ayer Hall, the first academic building erected on the Jackson State University campus, was built in 1903 and today houses the Margaret Walker Center, an archive and museum dedicated to the preservation, interpretation, and dissemination of African American history and culture.

JACKSON COLLEGE

Founded, October 23, 1877, by American Baptist Home Mission Society at Natchez. Removed to Jackson, 1882. Present site bought, 1902. Became a state teachers college for Negroes, 1940.

MISSISSIPPI HISTORICAL COMMISSION

**Jackson College
historic marker**

Florida Agricultural and Mechanical University

Florida Agricultural and Mechanical University (FAMU or Florida A&M), formerly known as the State Normal College for Colored Students, was founded in Tallahassee in 1887. FAMU is an 1890 land-grant research institution that remains devoted to the success of its undergraduate, graduate, doctoral, and professional students. Since its inception, FAMU has empowered communities through innovative research, teaching, and scholarship.

Florida A&M University Marching "100" orange drum major uniform, 1987

–

From 1946 to 1998, Dr. William P. Foster directed Florida A&M's Marching "100." Under Foster's leadership, the band combined traditional marching techniques with exciting interpretations of Black popular music and dance. The band often appears on television, in films, and in commercials and has performed at events around the United States and the world, including both of President Bill Clinton's inaugural parades in 1993 and 1997, the Walt Disney World national anniversary telecasts in 1986 and 1996, and the 1989 Bastille Day Parade in Paris, France, celebrating the bicentennial of the French Revolution as America's official representative.

Florida A&M Marching "100" performing during the Louis Vuitton Men's Fashion Show at the Louvre in Paris, France, June 2022
Tony Leavell

Dorothy Porter
Revolutionizing the Records

Dorothy Berry
Digital Curator, Office of Digital Strategy and Engagement, NMAAHC

Dorothy Porter (1905–1995) was the first Black graduate of Columbia University's library school and the organizer of what is now Howard University's Moorland-Spingarn Research Center. Her work to bring African American history and culture to light exemplifies her intellectual influence and the powerful service of librarians and archivists at Historically Black Colleges and Universities across the United States.

Porter became a librarian at Howard in 1930 and spent the next four decades quietly revolutionizing how people thought of and accessed African American collections. Her title of "librarian" encompassed many roles: cataloguer, bibliographer, collector, reference expert. In each of these roles, Porter completed groundbreaking work that remains influential to this day. She is perhaps most known as an innovator in what contemporary library science might refer to as "reparative cataloguing"—changing the way materials are classified to make them more accurate and more discoverable.

While building a collection at Howard covering subjects on Black life—from politics to literature to sociology and everything in between—Porter faced a system that made it impossible to classify the abundance of information on these topics. In Porter's day, patrons found library materials using card catalogues—vast shelves of narrow drawers stocked with little cards that held information about where to find books on different subjects, all based on the nationwide Dewey Decimal Classification. Porter found that this system offered official subjects relating to African Americans as soldiers and minstrels but very little else.

Unwilling to simplify her collecting and compromise service to her researchers, Porter used her library science education to complete a vast, unauthorized adaptation of the Dewey system. She redefined the categories under "History" to distinctly

"Black archivists ... have always taken a stand against injustice, oppression, and the whitewashing of the historical record ... censorship of books by and about Black people is on the rise, and access to information continues to be politicized and criminalized."

—Barrye Brown, curator, Manuscripts, Archives, and Rare Books Division, Schomburg Center for Research in Black Culture, 2024

Dorothy Porter instructing manuscript staff Thomas Battle, Evelyn Brooks-Barnett, and Denise Glelin, Howard University, 1974

focus on African American history: Dewey's category "War of Secession" became Porter's "The Negro During the Civil War." This reorganization was complicated intellectual work and professionally risky. The editor of the Dewey organization threatened Porter with the possibility of a copyright lawsuit if she published her unauthorized system, but this did not stop her from finding quiet methods to share her work with other HBCU librarians and archivists. A colleague published the system in her dissertation, and a librarian from the Schomburg Center for Research in Black Culture came to Washington from Harlem and learned the system in person. Finally, Porter inserted her system into a published *Catalogue of Books in the Moorland Foundation*, allowing colleagues across the country perpetual access to more deep and accurate ways of classifying their collections.

Porter's radical reimagining of the Dewey system may be her most well-known accomplishment, but it is certainly far from being her only. She advised the US War Department during World War II on books to send to Black soldiers, produced surveys and bibliographies of early African American publications, and collected archival materials from literary events, including the 1973 Phillis Wheatley Poetry Festival at Jackson State University. She even took redirected reference questions from the Library of Congress when their staff lacked knowledge of African American history and culture. Perhaps her greatest achievement, however, was her mentorship of future generations. Dorothy Porter remains a major influence on Black librarians and archivists, and her work at Howard University is an international inspiration.

NO LESS LOVELY BEING DARK
Capturing and Creating Beauty

The night whose sable breast relieves the stark,
White stars is no less lovely being dark,
And there are buds that cannot bloom at all
In light, but crumple, piteous, and fall.
So in the dark we hide the heart that bleeds,
And wait, and tend our agonizing seeds.
—Countee Cullen, excerpt "From the Dark Tower" (1926)

The poetic language of early twentieth-century Black poets may sound hopelessly quaint to the contemporary ear. Countee Cullen and his contemporaries employed phrases such as "no less lovely being dark" in a literary convention undergirded by lives that were far from quaint, delicate, or easy. A deeper parsing of Cullen's language reveals the power and poignancy of a people "not made eternally to weep," as Cullen wrote about Black life at a time when its price was dearly guarded, and its mere existence was challenged regularly.

Nowhere were the yearnings and strivings spoken of by Cullen more eloquently expressed than in the arts at Historically Black Colleges and Universities (HBCUs). The collections of art, literature, theater, and musical history housed in the museums, libraries, and archives at HBCUs, such as Clark Atlanta, Jackson State, Florida A&M, Texas Southern, and Tuskegee Universities, reveal the profound beauty and complex meaning that limned the lives of Americans, who were no less lovely being dark and no less eloquent being African American. That such artistic yearnings found fertile soil in these schools, despite the nation's deeply entrenched racial barriers, is a testament to these institutions' resilience and resolute spirit.

As HBCUs commemorate decades, and in some cases centuries, of educational excellence, it is a time and a cause for celebration. The murals of Hale Woodruff (1900–1980) at Clark Atlanta's Trevor Arnett Library, the African-inspired creations of painter and educator John Biggers (1924–2001) at Texas Southern, and the photographs of P. H. Polk at Tuskegee continue that tradition of excellence, for they represent the finest artifactual evidence in word and art for current and promised generations of African Americans and a larger public.

The high-stepping FAMU marching band, the Marching "100," is

Art of the Negro: Native Forms, 1950–51 (detail)
Hale Woodruff

emblematic of the performing-arts tradition in these schools, a tradition that embraces style, precision, and full-throated joy. Renowned sculptor Elizabeth Catlett fashioned engaging works, such as her bronze bust of the eighteenth-century poet Phillis Wheatley, which embodies the profound longings of Black life (p. 52). Catlett created this work of enduring beauty for display at Jackson State's 1973 Phillis Wheatley Poetry Festival.

The writers gathered at the poetry festival were, then and later, some of the most promising and celebrated poets, writers, and visual artists in American letters. Their names still resonate and their own influence models that of their enslaved but lettered muse, inspiring new generations of creative voices. The convener of that gathering, the writer and poet Margaret Walker (1915–1998), articulated the belief that the aspirations of Black people were joined in an inextricable web of common purpose and devotion, as she wrote in her germinal poem "For My People," first published in the November 1937 issue of *Poetry* magazine. Walker's words speak of an unshakable belief in the primacy of hope over despair, possibility over defeat:

For my people standing staring
trying to fashion a better way
from confusion, from hypocrisy and misunderstanding,
trying to fashion a world that will hold all the people,
all the faces, all the adams and eves and their countless generations.

Like Countee Cullen, Black poets before and during the early twentieth century crafted literary language that may sound anachronistic to the modern ear. Yet these writers, who broke through the legal barriers and miasma of racism, expressed a bedrock belief in the beauty, eloquence, and artistic talents of Black people. Their words reveal imaginative explorations that have lifted generations to lives lived in dignity and achievement in the face of extraordinary odds.

Kinshasha Holman Conwill
Deputy Director Emerita, NMAAHC

For My People, 1942
Margaret Walker

FOR MY PEOPLE

BY Margaret Walker

FOREWORD BY
Stephen Vincent Benét

Yale Series of Younger Poets

Friends, 1942
Margaret T. Burroughs

Art of the Negro: Native Forms, 1950–51
Hale Woodruff
–
Numerous HBCUs feature murals on their campuses. This creative tradition demonstrates the influence of early twentieth-century Mexican art traditions. While a professor at Atlanta University, Hale Woodruff spent a summer studying with Mexican muralist Diego Rivera in 1936. In the early 1950s, he translated these skills into the eight-panel mural series *Art of the Negro* at Atlanta University.

FAMU Spirit, 1973

**Trumpet used by the
Florida A&M University
Marching "100,"**
mid-20th century

Nubia, the Origins of Business and Commerce, 1991
John Biggers and
Harvey L. Johnson

Untitled, 2023
Franck Kemkeng Noah
–
Cameroonian artist Franck Kemkeng Noah created and performed in this sculptural costume while a teaching resident artist at Texas Southern University in 2023. He mentored TSU art students as part of his residency. Noah's art blends his Cameroonian cultural background with the European and American contexts in which he has worked. Though primarily a painter, Noah used his residency to explore working with sculpture. This work, using found objects collected during travels around the world, is a coat inspired by traditional masks of Cameroon.

String quartet, ca. 1932
P. H. Polk
-

P. H. Polk was Tuskegee University's official photographer for forty years. He was among the first students to enroll in the school's newly founded photography department in the early 1900s. There, he trained under C. M. Battey, the school's previous photographer.

Tuskegee Institute Dance, 1947
P. H. Polk

ALL THE SWEEP AND GRANDEUR
OF **GONE WITH THE WIND!**
THE SENSATIONAL NEW NOVEL
OF THE OLD SOUTH...

JUBILEE

BY MARGARET WALKER
A HOUGHTON MIFFLIN LITERARY
FELLOWSHIP AWARD NOVEL

11080-2 ★ $1.95 ★ A BANTAM BOOK

Jubilee, 1966
Margaret Walker

Margaret Walker signing *Jubilee*, 1966
–

Margaret Walker became a leading literary figure in Chicago in the 1930s, garnering national attention as a poet. Walker's acclaimed novel *Jubilee*, which depicts the life of an enslaved family in the South during the Civil War, took over twenty years to write. Upon receiving a book contract, she wrote in her personal journal, "The dream of a lifetime is coming true . . . Hooray! And thank God!"

Phillis Wheatley, 1973
Elizabeth Catlett
–

As a career educator at Jackson State University, Margaret Walker promoted African American literature by publishing and organizing major literary events that hosted other writers, educators, and students. In 1973, JSU's Phillis Wheatley Poetry Festival brought together twenty-three nationally recognized African American women poets to celebrate the work of the enslaved eighteenth-century poet and discuss what it meant to be a woman writer during the 1960s and 70s. Sculptor Elizabeth Catlett created this bronze bust of Phillis Wheatley for the 1973 poetry festival named in Wheatley's honor. The bust depicted here resides in the NMAAHC's collection, while an identical bust is housed at Jackson State.

Women writers at the Phillis Wheatley Poetry Festival, Jackson State University Botanical Garden, 1973
Roy Lewis
–

Left to right: Margaret Burroughs, Marion Alexander, June Jordan, Dorothy Porter, Audre Lorde, Mari Evans, Malaika Wangara,

Etta Moten Barnett, Paula Giddings, Alice Walker, Doris Saunders, Gloria Oden, Margaret Danner, Linda Bragg, Carole Clemmons.

A MIND IS A MARVELOUS THING
Intellectual and Academic Development

The emergence of Historically Black Colleges and Universities (HBCUs) was revolutionary from the start. Prior to 1865, providing access to literacy skills and a formal education to any Black person was illegal in many areas of the United States. Nevertheless, in 1837, the Institute for Colored Youth in Philadelphia, subsequently renamed Cheney University, was the first in a long and proud line of HBCUs to be established to serve the needs of African Americans, recognizing the correlation between education and racial equality.

By 1865, in the aftermath of the American Civil War, a battle-torn nation began the process of rebuilding as newly emancipated and free-born Black citizens began navigating the concept of freedom. Yet, the struggle to combat racialized oppression persisted, making the freedom to learn and pursue formal education a primary path to social and economic liberation.

Two prominent nineteenth-century thought leaders, Booker T. Washington and William Edward Burghardt (W. E. B.) Du Bois, worked to imbue African descendant people with a sense of identity, accomplishment, and cultural pride. Hampton alumnus Booker T. Washington (1856–1915) was an author and educator who founded the Tuskegee Institute (later renamed

Tuskegee University). W. E. B. Du Bois (1868–1963), famed scholar and historian, began his college education in 1885 at Fisk University and later transferred to Harvard College, becoming the school's first African American to receive a PhD. Du Bois later served as a sociology professor at Atlanta University (now Clark Atlanta University).

Their achievements were embodied by a new generation of pioneering educators and HBCU faculty, such as renowned scholar, author, and humanitarian George Washington Carver (1864–1943). As the first African American to receive an advanced degree in agricultural science, Carver was already a foremost scholar when Booker T. Washington recruited him to lead the Tuskegee Institute's agricultural department, wherein he designed the Jesup Wagon, a mobile classroom used to provide hands-on agricultural education to tenant farmers and sharecroppers.

Similarly, Dr. Jane Ellen McAllister, a Talladega College alumna who was always ahead of her time, became the first African American woman in the United States to earn a PhD in education in 1929. That remarkable achievement was merely a prelude to a career devoted to empowering

Students in Atlanta University's Trevor Arnett Library Rotunda, ca. 1955 (detail)

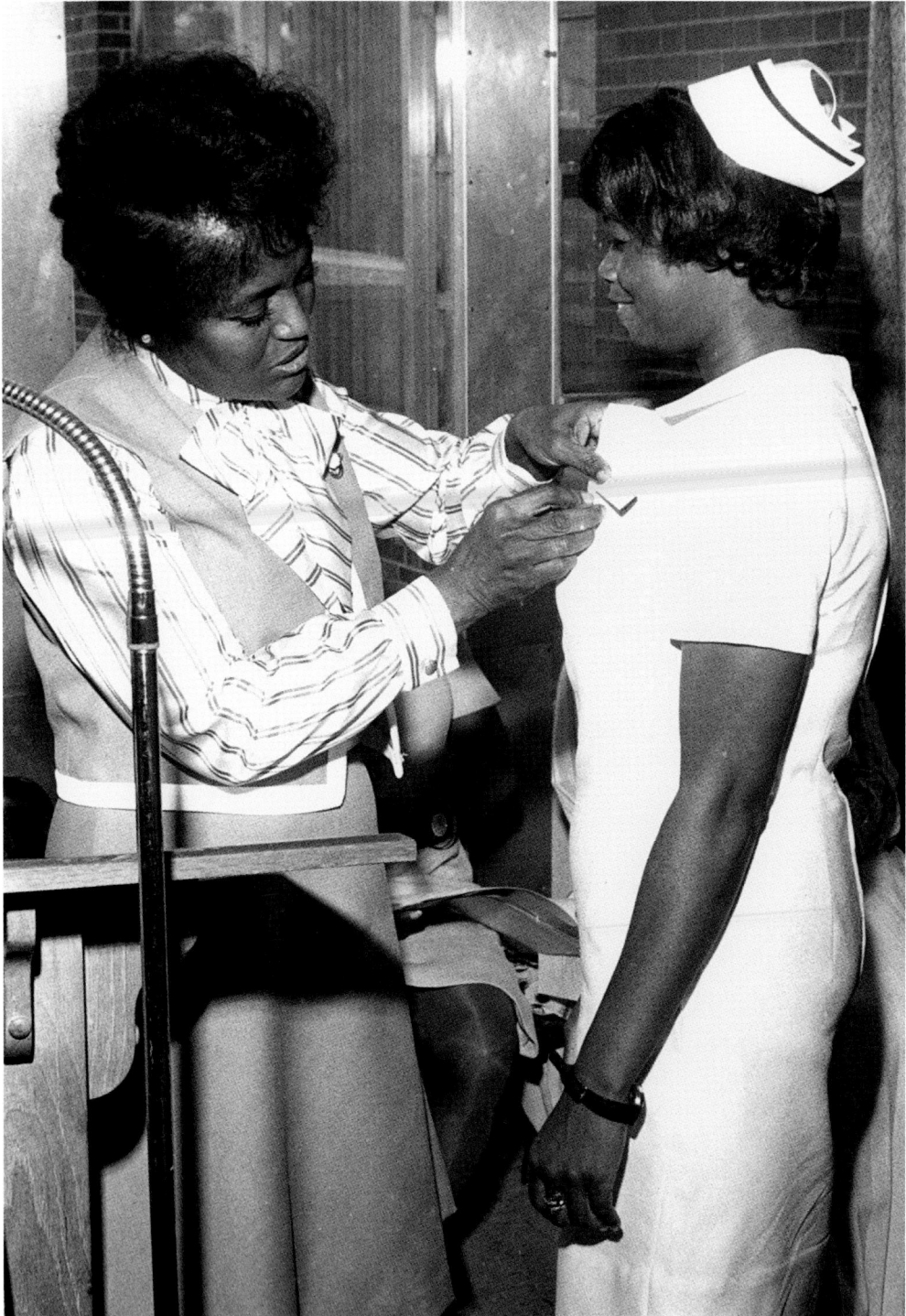

others, by teaching Black youth, helping establish community schools, and working as a consultant to the Rosenwald Fund. During her fifteen-year tenure at Jackson State, she trained generations of Black teachers, and throughout her career, she published extensive research on teacher education.

Under the leadership and skilled coaching of Dr. Thomas Freeman (1919–2020), the Texas Southern University debate team rose to national and international prominence. Beginning in 1949, Freeman dedicated eight decades of his career to the university and to all students committed to honing their critical thinking, speaking, and writing skills through college debate competitions. At these debates, students won many awards and trophies for their academic excellence.

Throughout the twentieth century, HBCUs expanded their reach by advancing social, political, and economic opportunities, offering African Americans unparalleled professional training and skill development in an array of disciplines that equip students for success. Generations of educators have helped to advance Tuskegee's renowned agricultural science and architecture studies; Florida A&M's incomparable agroecology, business, and nursing programs;

and Jackson State's excellent education, Black studies, and biochemistry departments. They have developed exceptional courses in art education and library science programs at Clark Atlanta and unparalleled studies in languages and visual arts at Texas Southern. Like all HBCUs, these venerable institutions have made an immense impact on the academy, students, and communities they serve.

In the twenty-first century, HBCUs continue equipping nimble minds to learn, compete, and excel no matter their chosen profession. The professionals and knowledgeable practitioners who helped establish America's Black middle class are living testaments to the relevance and effectiveness of HBCUs in consistently producing the highest number of Black graduates in every academic discipline. For over 150 years, HBCUs have molded and prepared successive generations of innovators, thought leaders, and changemakers to make a meaningful impact on society.

Marion McGee
Program Partnership Manager, Office of Strategic Partnerships, NMAAHC

Graduation ceremony of Florida A&M nursing student Lawana Simmons, 1960s–70s

Bust of W. E. B. Du Bois (2013) by Ayokunle Odeleye on the Clark Atlanta Campus, 2016
Kevin Coles
–

Although Booker T. Washington and W. E. B. Du Bois both emphasized the importance of education for African Americans, their differing philosophies shaped the course of African American education in the early twentieth century. Washington, who ran the Tuskegee Institute from 1881 to 1915, promoted vocational education at HBCUs, believing that practical training in areas such as agriculture and mechanics would help African Americans to obtain respect and rise in social status. In contrast, Du Bois, who taught at Atlanta University from 1897 to 1910, championed the liberal arts, arguing that an education focused on the classics, arts, and humanities would prepare African Americans to lead the fight for civil rights and social change. Despite their ideological differences, the impact of Washington and Du Bois's leadership in establishing spaces for Black intellectual pursuits and pathbreaking literary publications is most evident in their shared impact on subsequent generations of Black scholars, educators, and cultural preservationists.

**The Booker T. Washington
Monument, *Lifting the Veil of
Ignorance (1922)*, by sculptor
Charles Keck on the Tuskegee
University Campus**

Jackson State graduate student observing outcomes of an experiment, 2021
-

HBCUs are vital to advancing the nation's public health. Over the past 150 years, they have been leaders in educating primary care physicians, conducting groundbreaking scientific research, and elevating health in underserved communities. Through their collaborations and partnerships with national health care and awareness institutions, they have strengthened their efforts to help ensure quality health care for all United States citizens.

Jeanne M. Walton examines HeLa cells used in the development of a polio vaccine at Tuskegee, 1950s

Walter T. Bailey instructing students with architectural drawing exhibits, 1906
Frances Benjamin Johnston

Students in Atlanta University's Trevor Arnett Library Rotunda, ca. 1955
–

Hale Woodruff's *Art of the Negro* murals can be seen high on the walls behind the students.

Jesup Agricultural Wagon, early 1900s
–

During his forty-seven years at Tuskegee from 1896 to 1943, George Washington Carver developed the agriculture department into a powerhouse research center. In his garden, he experimented with various crops and tested different farming methods. These methods helped farmers improve the quality of their crops and livestock. Through his rural extension work, he helped farmers increase their crop yield by explaining the benefits of fertilization and crop rotation to restore nutrients to the soil.

Building on Carver's rural extension work, Booker T. Washington conceived the idea of a movable wagon to introduce new farming techniques and products and to inspire farmers struggling economically on poorly cultivated land. In 1906, Carver sketched a wagon and drafted detailed plans to implement Washington's idea. This first moveable school would be called the Jesup Agricultural Wagon, named after benefactor Morris K. Jesup. The wagon transported exhibits and items such as farming utensils, machinery, fertilizer, seeds, and vegetables to small and large farms, and the demonstration agent explained their effective use.

The Booker T. Washington Agricultural School on Wheels, ca. 1930
–

In 1923 a third moveable school was built and named in honor of Tuskegee Institute's founding principal Booker T. Washington. The Booker T. Washington Agricultural School on Wheels facilitated the expansion of the extension program's work by including home care and practical life skills, with the added ability to serve communities not only across the region but also in surrounding states.

Jackson College teachers in a classroom with young students, 1954
–

Dr. Jane Ellen McAllister—the first African American woman to earn a doctorate in education—established Jackson State University's teacher training program. At Jackson State, Dr. McAllister revolutionized the institution's educational offerings, most notably directing the Jackson State College Summer Project Enrichment Program for teachers and high school students, creating partnerships between the college and rural school districts across the state, and developing a college readiness program for college freshmen, among a host of other initiatives.

Dr. Jane Ellen McAllister, 1940

Texas Southern University Debate Team, ca. 1956
–
Left to right: Donald Anderson, Otis King, Dr. Thomas Freeman (coach), Barbara Jordan (future US congresswoman), Prentiss Moore.

First-place trophy in Junior Women's Oratory awarded to the Texas Southern University Debate Team at the Baylor Forensic competition, 1967
–
Debate teams at HBCUs served dual purposes. They helped to counter notions of African American intellectual inferiority, and they were training grounds for future leaders. Texas Southern University's debate team, Sigma Pi Alpha, has been winning competitions since its founding in 1949 by Dr. Thomas Freeman. Under Dr. Freeman's leadership for more than sixty years, the TSU debate team rose to national prominence.

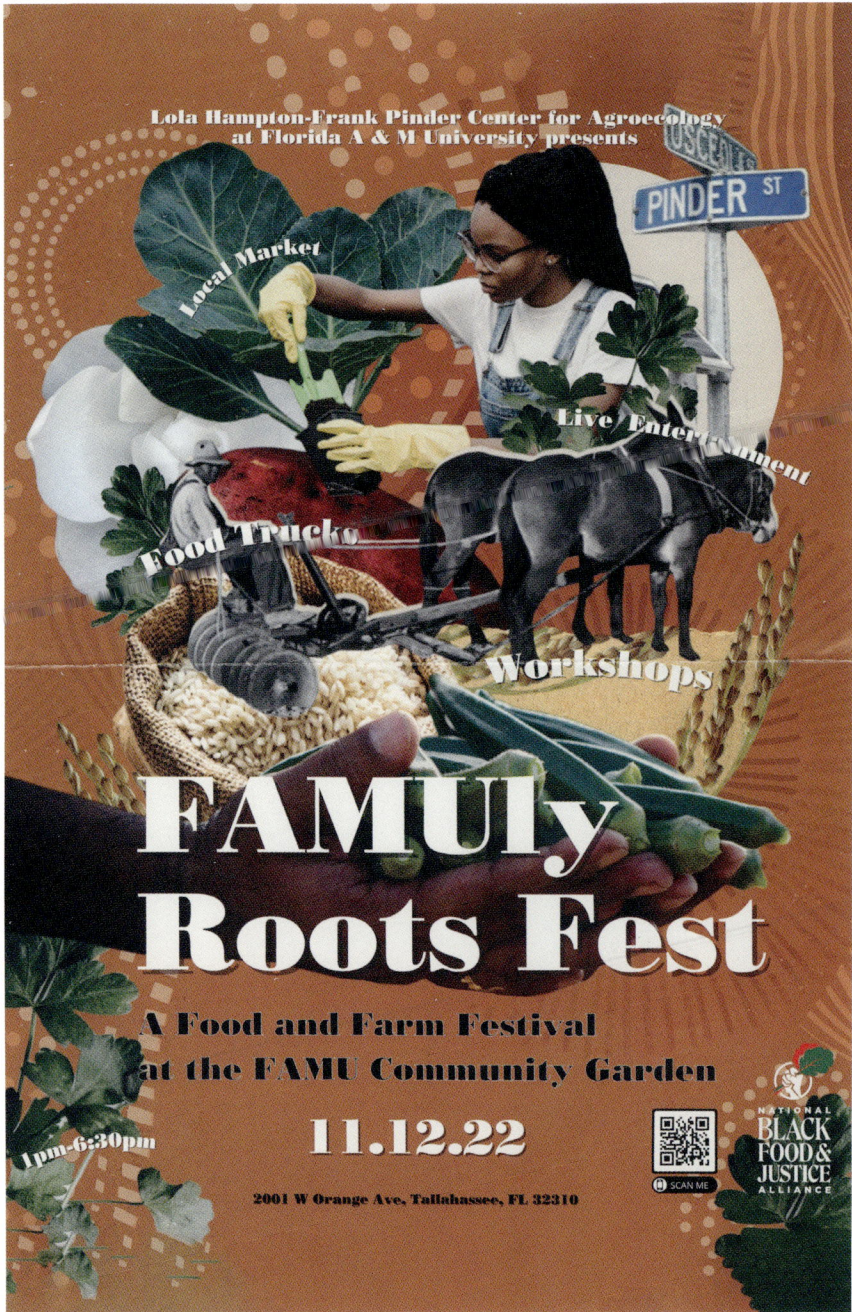

Lola Hampton-Frank Pinder Center for Agroecology at Florida A & M University presents

Local Market

Live Entertainment

Food Trucks

Workshops

FAMUly Roots Fest

A Food and Farm Festival at the FAMU Community Garden

11.12.22

1pm-6:30pm

2001 W Orange Ave, Tallahassee, FL 32310

SCAN ME

NATIONAL BLACK FOOD & JUSTICE ALLIANCE

Flyer for FAMUly Roots Fest celebrating the Lola Hampton-Frank Pinder Center for Agroecology, 2022
–
Named after Lola Hampton and Frank Pinder—two Black land stewards from Tallahassee—Florida A&M University's Lola Hampton-Frank Pinder Center for Agroecology builds upon the university's extension program and history of providing resources to Black farmers. Since 2022, the Center for Agroecology has worked to support and preserve Black farming communities by centering Black farmers' voices, knowledge, skills, and strategies in their work. The Center's rootedness in agroecology illustrates their commitment to fostering sustainable agricultural practices and healing communities through healthy food and farming practices.

Vonda Richardson, Executive Director of FAMU's Cooperative Extension program, at a community garden event, West Palm Beach, Florida, 2022

Data Power
Monroe and Florence Work's Meticulous Efforts Documenting Black Life, 1900–1945

Jeanelle K. Hope
Caterpillar Curator of Innovation and Entrepreneurship, NMAAHC

Monroe Nathan Work was born August 15, 1866, to formerly enslaved parents in Iredell County, North Carolina. After spending much of his youth supporting his family, Work belatedly began high school at 23. By 1898 he had enrolled in the sociology program at the University of Chicago; he was among the first African Americans to graduate from the institution. During his tenure in Chicago, Work began conducting research on African American communities in the area, culminating with the publication of "Crime Among the Negroes of Chicago: A Social Study" in the *American Journal of Sociology*—the journal's first publication by an African American. Published in 1900, this article showcased Work's approach to research, which incorporated statistical data, ethnography, and archival research, among other methods, and refuted racially biased studies like Frederick Hoffman's *Race Traits and Tendencies of the American Negro*. While Hoffman and other white researchers studying Black people during the era often used their research to amplify eugenic theory, Work's research provided more nuance and fuller accounts of African American progress.

In 1904, just one year after completing his master's degree, Monroe Work married Florence Hendrickson. They initially settled in Georgia, where Monroe served on the faculty at Georgia State Industrial College for Colored Youth in Savannah (now Savannah State University). He worked closely with another prominent African American sociologist, W. E. B. Du Bois, helping to advance the anti-segregation lobbying work of the Niagara Movement. The Works' time in Savannah would be short-lived, as Monroe soon received an offer from Booker T. Washington that would further elevate his research.

In 1908, Monroe Work was appointed by Booker T. Washington to serve as the institution's inaugural director of the Department of Records and Research, where he was commissioned to supply data on African American life to support Washington's speeches and writings. Furthermore, he was tasked with collecting information on the first generations of Tuskegee Institute students and alumni, which would later be published as *Industrial Work of Tuskegee Graduates and Former Students During the Year 1910*. And his early research on African American health outcomes was used to promote Washington's brainchild event, National Negro Health Week.

As Monroe Work's research scope and readership grew, Florence Work became more involved in helping compile data and review writings. Building upon Ida B. Wells-Barnett's seminal reports on lynchings during the era, in 1910 the Works began producing lynching reports that were published in the *Chicago Herald*. This data on lynchings was among the most widely disseminated at the time, and today Tuskegee University maintains one of the most comprehensive archives on lynchings in the United States because of the Works' efforts. However, one of their most audacious and pioneering projects would be the publication of nine editions of the *Negro Year Book*—a periodical of encyclopedic facts, organizations, and major events related to African American life.

Throughout his career at Tuskegee, Monroe Work held the belief that "facts will help eradicate prejudice and

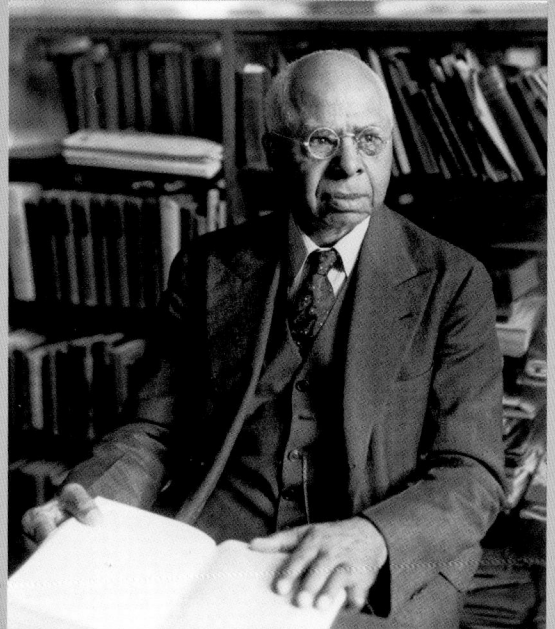

Monroe Work, 1930s
C. M. Battey

misunderstanding . . . for facts are the truth and the truth shall set us free." This motto motivated Monroe and Florence Work to develop a powerhouse Department of Records and Research and archive of data on African American life that continue to inform the work of scholars today.

DOING BATTLE WHERE WE STAND

Student-Led Activism and Radical Reform

Florida A&M University (FAMU) president Nathan Young delivered an address before the school in 1915 entitled "Militant Citizenship." His speech leaned into a long tradition of fostering civic engagement that Historically Black Colleges and Universities (HBCUs) adopted since their inception in the early nineteenth century. Indeed, one of Black colleges' most significant offerings to America has been the cultivation of militant citizenship that launched the most important social movements in our nation's history.

In states like Florida, HBCUs offered a "shelter in a time of storm." Radical mentorship from administrators like Nathan Young and the dedicated faculty he recruited resulted in generations of students at FAMU assuming their role as change agents. Students boycotted classes when the state-appointed "Board of Control" forced Young out of his position in 1923. As the modern Civil Rights Movement unfolded, FAMU students used that same resolve to

launch the Tallahassee Bus Boycott in 1956, engage in lunch-counter sit-ins in 1960, and clog the jails and courts in 1963 in protest against segregation.

During the sit-ins of 1960, Clark Atlanta University served as a hub of activity. Students from Clark College and Atlanta University (the two institutions merged in 1988) fused intellectualism and idealism with the new student-led protests. Atlanta University president Dr. Rufus Clement encouraged students to compose their manifesto entitled *An Appeal for Human Rights*, which was published in local newspapers and eventually the *New York Times*. Clement himself helped to raise the money to publish the students' declaration. The Atlanta Student Movement became a model for student-led insurgency across the nation.

Concerns about racial violence targeting students was among several reasons that certain HBCU presidents obstructed activism on their campuses.

"The battle of Negro students for freedom here is really an attempt to free the entire region from the irrational terror that has ruled it for so long."

—James Baldwin, in "They Can't Turn Back," *Mademoiselle* magazine, August 1960, reporting from FAMU on student protests

Untitled,
ca. 1975 (detail)
Edward Mills

This violence tragically manifested itself in the murder of activist and Tuskegee college student Sammy Younge Jr. on January 3, 1966. Younge was tragically gunned down at a Macon County, Alabama, gas station following a verbal altercation with the station attendant. In the trial that followed, an all-white jury pronounced Younge's assailant not guilty.

On May 16, 1967, students at Texas Southern University (TSU) in Houston participated in a protest against environmental racism by calling for the closure of city dumps that were placed in Black neighborhoods. Local police invaded the institution and opened fire on the campus. By the end of the day, 488 TSU students were arrested and five were charged with the murder of a Houston police officer. Charges against the students were dropped after an investigation revealed their innocence. No TSU students were killed during the raid.

In Jackson, Mississippi, tension surged as the forces of white supremacy claimed the lives of movement activists in the city and around the state. Those sentiments swelled once again following the 1967 police shooting of twenty-one-year-old Benjamin Brown, a Jackson State University student. The tension reached a climax on May 15, 1970, after police opened fire on the campus, killing JSU student Phillip Gibbs and local high school student James Green. No one was ever prosecuted for the murders of Brown, Gibbs, or Green.

The collective histories of these institutions illustrate how HBCUs cultivated militant citizenship that profoundly altered the trajectory of America. Despite continuous underfunding and external and internal efforts to undermine these spaces as seedbeds of activism, Black colleges remain a significant wellspring of idealism that creates new paths toward a more just society and world.

Jelani M. Favors
Henry E. Frye Distinguished Professor of History and Director, Center of Excellence for Social Justice, North Carolina A&T State University

Untitled, ca. 1970s
Bennie Settles
–
Bennie Settles studied art at TSU in the 1970s and pursued a career in graphic design. In this painting, Settles depicts the violence frequently inflicted by police officers on Black men and the way that it impacts their neighbors and community.

FAMU students march to the state capitol to protest a proposal to merge with Florida State University, ca. 1967

Flyer for a student mass rally at Trevor Arnett Library sponsored by the Student Nonviolent Coordinating Committee, 1964

-

Legal action and support of legal action was one of the many tactics used to target and end segregation during the Civil Rights Movement. Though Title II of the 1964 Civil Rights Act ended racial discrimination in restaurants, hotels, theaters, and other types of public accommodations, student activists tested and picketed those businesses that did not adhere to the law.

VF   Student   Non-violent   Coordinating   Committee

WE DEMAND

IMMEDIATE RELEASE OF DEMONSTRATORS

PASSAGE OF A PUBLIC ACCOMMODATIONS LAW

NO MORE ARRESTS OF PEACEFUL DEMONSTRATORS

TREVOR ARNETT LIBRARY

TUES. JAN. 28   2.30 P.M.

MASS RALLY

SNCC COAHR

Atlanta Mural, 1976
Romare Bearden
–

Romare Bearden made this maquette for an unrealized ninety-six-foot mural that was designed to appear on the campus of Atlanta University. Bearden was a multi-media artist based in Harlem, New York, and a founding member, alongside former Atlanta University faculty member Hale Woodruff, of Spiral, a group focused on bringing to light the importance of art in the Civil Rights Movement. Along with the portrayal of a family, this maquette depicts Dr. Martin Luther King Jr., who became publicly vocal on civil rights as a student at Morehouse College in Atlanta.

"We want and are entitled to the basic rights and opportunities of American citizens ... [and] some of the same courtesy and good manners that we ourselves bring to all human relations."

–Dr. Martin Luther King Jr., in "Kick Up Dust," Letter to the Editor, *Atlanta Constitution* newspaper, August 6, 1946, written while a student at Morehouse College

Tuskegee student occupation of Dorothy Hall, April 6, 1968
P. H. Polk
–

Just two days after the assassination of Dr. Martin Luther King Jr., approximately three hundred students surrounded Dorothy Hall on Tuskegee's campus, where members of the Board of Trustees were holding a meeting. The students' demands included changes to financial aid and the creation of a Black studies program. Administrators eventually agreed to meet with the students, which led to the implementation of nearly all of their demands. The Tuskegee Uprising is an example of one of many instances where students on HBCU campuses successfully protested for the addition of Black studies programs on campus.

a. Afro-American History courses be added as options in general educational requirements.

b. Additional courses be added which include the following:

   1. Sociology of black people, i.e. problems of the black communities--indepth courses--and course in the Black Family structure and function.

   2. Social-Psychology of the Black man.

   3. Ibo and Swahili offered as foreign language requirements.

   4. African and Afro-American Literary Appreciation.

   5. An initiation of an African Studies Program.

   6. Emphasis in all Social Science disciplines related to, and as a frame of reference, the Black experience pertaining specifically to economics, sociology, history, anthropology and related arts.

   7. Increased teaching staff to meet the needs for putting the above proposals into effective operation.

List of Black studies courses proposed by students at Tuskegee from *Student Unrest, Tuskegee Institute, A Chronology*, 1968 Chester Higgins Jr.
–

Tuskegee students proposed a Black studies curriculum designed to expand student and faculty self-knowledge and understanding of African and African American history and culture. General education requirements, such as the social sciences, would be viewed through the lens of the African American experience and emphasis would be placed on African languages and history as well as Black literature.

Untitled, ca. 1975
Edward Mills
-

Edward Mills grew up in Houston, Texas, and studied art education at TSU in the 1960s. This mural, which depicts an American flag and events of the 1960s Black Freedom Movement at TSU and around the United States, is one of forty student murals on display in TSU's historic Mack H. Hannah Hall.

Frankye Adams's pinback buttons, 1960-90s

–

These lapel pins belonged to Frankye "Malika" Adams, an activist and career educator at Jackson State University. In the 1960s, as a student at Tougaloo College in Mississippi, Adams became actively involved with Student Nonviolent Coordinating Committee, the Freedom Riders, and the March on Washington. In 1967, she left Mississippi for New York, where she joined the Black Panther Party as a community organizer. These lapel pins are emblematic of her commitment to bringing about radical reform in the United States.

BLACK PANTHER
NEWSPAPER COMMITTEE

BIRMINGHAM, ALABAMA
1963
FOOT SOLDIERS
INSPIRED BY WHAT WE DID FOR OURSELVES - AND THE WORLD
REUNION

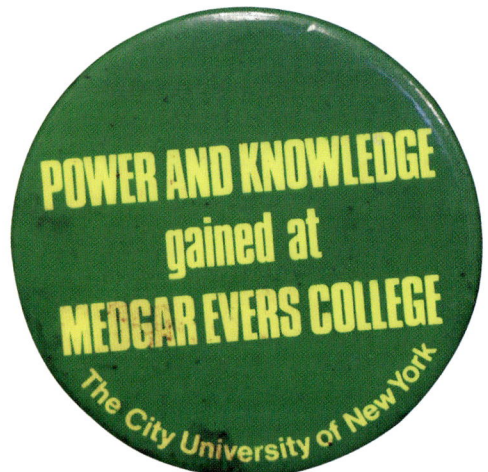

POWER AND KNOWLEDGE
gained at
MEDGAR EVERS COLLEGE
The City University of New York

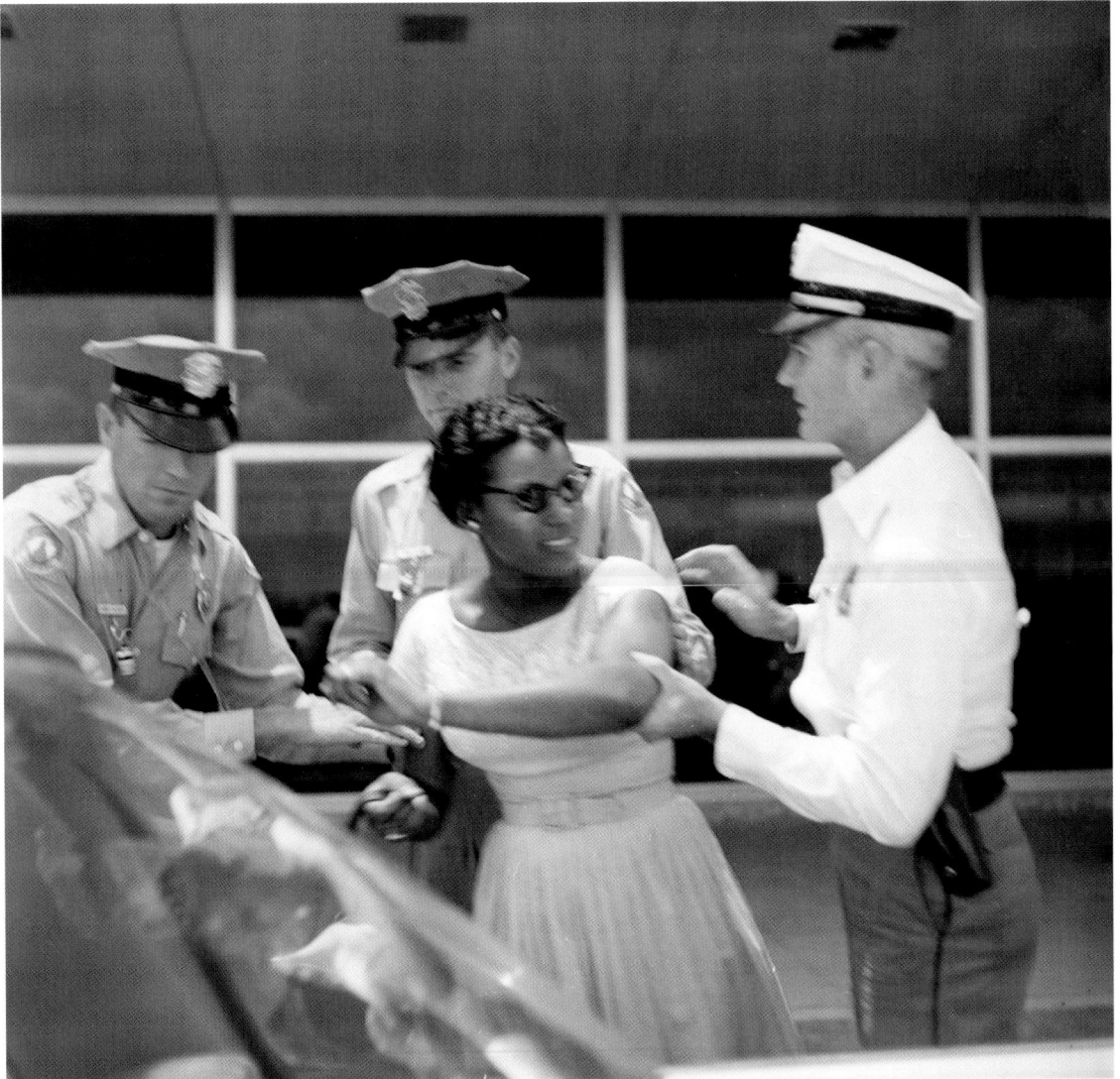

Priscilla Stephens being arrested at the Tallahassee Regional Airport, 1961
-

Priscilla Stephens and her sister, Patricia, founded the Tallahassee chapter of the Congress of Racial Equality (CORE) and used support from the national organization to protest segregation and discrimination in Florida. When arrested, many FAMU students refused to pay bail, leading to some of the first "jail-ins" in Civil Rights history.

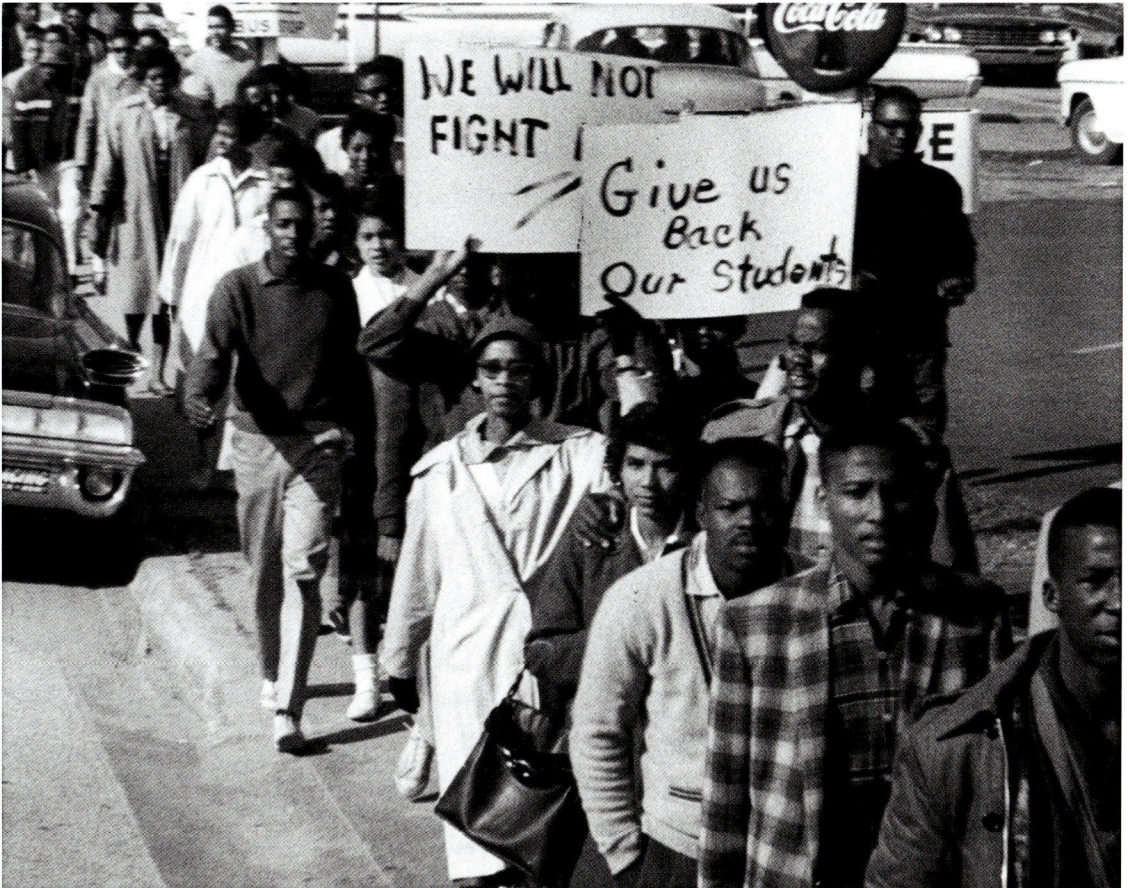

FAMU students on a protest march, Tallahassee, Florida, 1960

"Every night before I go to sleep I thank God that in some small way that I am able to help those of us who are denied our equal rights. I do not consider going to jail a sacrifice but a privilege."

—Priscilla Stephens, draft of a letter written while in Leon County Jail, 1960

FAMU students hold a sit-in protest in the rotunda of the Florida State Capitol to protest the results of the 2000 presidential election in Florida, November 2000

–

On November 9, 2000, just two days after the controversial 2000 presidential election between George W. Bush and Al Gore, nearly 2,500 Florida A&M students marched from the university campus to the State Capitol to protest discrepancies in the vote count, election results, and voter intimidation experienced at the polls. Over 250 student activists stayed in the capitol rotunda overnight, sleeping outside the offices of Governor Jeb Bush and Secretary of State Katherine Harris. The students remained in the capitol for nearly twenty-four hours, staging a sit-in while calling for an investigation of ballot irregularities, cancelled vote counts in majority-minority counties, and a subsequent re-count of select ballots throughout Florida.

TSU student protest,
March 2021
–

Members of the TSU debate team and student government, led by Brittney Sheppard, Nahab Fahnbulleh, and Khaniya Burley, march down Cleburne Street to commemorate the March 1960 sit-in led by Texas Southern students at Weingarten's grocery store that led to the desegregation of public places in Houston.

Pickets, 1946
Roy DeCarava

Young Americans Series: Tarrynn Deavens, age 18, African American, 2007
Sheila Pree Bright
–
Sheila Pree Bright's *Young Americans* series examines the values and attitudes of millennials, regarding their American identity. Bright captures her subjects with an American flag in positions of their own choice. While Tarrynn Deavens, a student at Hampton University, is pictured as restrained by the flag, other subjects wear the flag as a cape or a blanket. This is one of many contemporary works in the Clark Atlanta University Art Museum and signals the direction the museum is taking with collecting the present and the future of African American art.

ACKNOWLEDGMENTS

Along with the *At the Vanguard* exhibition, this engaging companion publication is the vision of so many whose support and talents made this project a reality. The gratifying work of highlighting HBCU collections will help ensure their preservation and vitality for future generations of students, researchers, and educators. The publication team cheerfully acknowledges and expresses its sincere gratitude to the following individuals for their contributions and unwavering commitment to this crucial work:

Smithsonian NMAAHC Leadership

Michelle Commander, Deputy Director
Deborah Mack, Associate Director, Office of Strategic Partnerships
Auntaneshia Staveloz, Project Director and Supervisory Program Manager, Office of Strategic Partnerships

At the Vanguard Publication

NMAAHC Publication Team

Tulani Salahu-Din, Series Editor and Museum Specialist, Language and Literature
Marion McGee, Volume Co-Editor and Program Partnership Manager, Office of Strategic Partnerships
Douglas Remley, Senior Editor/Publications Manager
Pauline Lopez, Licensing Contractor

Essay Contributors

Dorothy Berry, Digital Curator, NMAAHC
Kinshasha Holman Conwill, Deputy Director Emerita, NMAAHC
Jeanelle K. Hope, Caterpillar Curator of Innovation and Entrepreneurship, NMAAHC
Jelani M. Favors, Professor of History, North Carolina A&T State University

D. Giles Limited

Dan Giles, Managing Director
Alfonso Iacurci, Designer
Liz Japes, Sales Director
Allison McCormick, Managing Editor
Louise Ramsay, Production Director
Jodi Simpson, Copyeditor and Proofreader

At the Vanguard Exhibition

National Museum of African American History and Culture

Courtney Alexander, Student Intern, Clark Atlanta University
Mike Biddle, Exhibit Designer
Lydia Charles, Education Specialist
Shareen Dash, Supervisory Education Specialist
Atiya Dorsey, Curatorial Research Assistant
Julia Hirsch, Curatorial Assistant
Jeanelle K. Hope, Caterpillar Curator of Innovation and Entrepreneurship
Joanne Hyppolite, Museum Curator
Deborah Mack, Associate Director, Office of Strategic Partnerships
Laura Manaker, Project Manager
Ernesto Mendoza, Exhibit Designer
Cassidy Moses, Education Specialist
Tulani Salahu-Din, Museum Specialist, Language and Literature

Smithsonian Institution Traveling Exhibition Services

Carol Bossert, Director Exhibition Program
Christina Brownlee, Registrar
Marquette Folley, Content Director
Alyssa Hockenberry, Registrar

HBCU History and Culture Access Consortium Partners

Clark Atlanta University Museum

Danille Taylor, Director
Shyheim Williams, Digital Humanities Manager

Meek-Eaton Black Archives & Museum, Florida A&M University

Timothy Barber, Director
Barbara Twyman, Digital Humanities Manager

Margaret Walker Center, Jackson State University

Robert Luckett Jr., Director
R. Garrad Lee, Digital Humanities Manager

University Museum at Texas Southern

Alvia Wardlaw, Director
Ben Schachter, Digital Humanities Manager

Tuskegee University Archives

Dana Chandler, Director Emeritus
Cheryl Ferguson, Director
Marvin Byrd, Digital Humanities Manager

HBCU History and Culture Access Consortium Collaborators

Roy Rosenzweig Center for History and New Media, George Mason University

Laura Brannan Fretwell, Graduate
  Research Assistant
Luz A. Giraldo Mueller, Graduate
  Research Assistant
T. Mills Kelly, Professor and Project Director
  (2020-2024)
Timmia King, Graduate Research Assistant
Lincoln Mullen, Executive Director
Deepthi Murali, Assistant Professor and
  Project Director
Ashley Palazzo, Metadata Specialist
Amber Pelham, Graduate Research Assistant

Center for Digital Humanities, University of Arizona

Bryan Carter, Director
Tristin Anaya
Amelia Matheson
Ernest Walker IV
Cosmo Brusa Zappellini

The Compass Group

Robert Bull Jr., President/CEO
Brandon S. Fields, Senior Consultant

Dickerson Global Advisors

Amina Dickerson, President

HBCU History and Culture Access Consortium Supporters

The 14th Secretary of the Smithsonian and the
  Smithsonian National Board
Bank of America
Bequest from Dr. Beryl Carter Rice
Coldwell Banker Richard Ellis (CBRE)
Council on Library and Information
  Resources (CLIR)
Google Arts and Culture
Institute of Museum and Library Services
National Endowment for the Humanities
The TJX Companies, Inc.

Cover *tl*: Tuskegee University Archives, Tuskegee, Alabama; **Cover** *bl*: Courtesy of Florida Memory; **Cover** *r*: Permanent Collection, University Museum at Texas Southern; **2**: Tuskegee University Archives, Tuskegee, Alabama; **4-5**: Tuskegee University Archives, Tuskegee, Alabama; **6**: Atlanta University Photographs Collection, Atlanta University Center Robert W. Woodruff Library; **8**: Brandon Hogg, Salty Hogg Photography; **9**: Malcolm Heimdall, Heimdall Images, LLC; **10**: Collection of the Smithsonian National Museum of African American History and Culture, © 2025 Mora-Catlett Family/Licensed by VAGA at Artists Rights Society (ARS), NY, 2008.14; **13**: Leah L. Jones/NMAAHC; **14**: Tuskegee University Archives, Tuskegee, Alabama; **15**: Margaret Walker Center, Jackson State University; **19**: Jane Ellen McAllister Papers, courtesy David Rae Morris; **20**: Texas Southern University Archives and Special Collections; **22-23**: © Tony Leavell; **25**: Jackson State University/Getty Images; **26**: Tuskegee University Archives, Tuskegee, Alabama; **27**: Tuskegee University Archives, Tuskegee, Alabama; **28**: Atlanta University Photographs Collection, Atlanta University Center Robert W. Woodruff Library; **29**: Hale Woodruff (1900-1980), *The Yellow Bird*, 1951, Oil on canvas, 31.375 in. x 23.375 in. Clark Atlanta University Art Museum, First Atlanta University Purchase Award, Oils (Any Subject), 1951.003; **30**: University Museum at Texas Southern Archive; **31**: Permanent Collection, University Museum at Texas Southern; **32**: Jackson State University Division of University Communications; **33**: Margaret Walker Center, Jackson State University; **34**: Courtesy of the Marching "100" Collection, Meek-Eaton Black Archives & Museum, Florida A&M University; **35**: © Tony Leavell; **37**: Dorothy Porter Wesley Papers, Beinecke Rare Book and Manuscript Library; **38**: Hale Woodruff (1900-1980), *Art of the Negro: Native Forms*, 1950-51. Oil on Canvas, panel ⅙, 11 ft. x 11 ft. Clark Atlanta University Art Museum, University Commission, 1952.012; **41**: Margaret Walker Center, Jackson State University; **42**: Margaret T. Burroughs (1915-2010), *Friends*, 1945. Lithograph. 14.875 in. x 9 in. Clark Atlanta University Art Museum, Third Atlanta University Purchase Award, Prints (Graphics), 1945.011; **43**: Hale Woodruff (1900-1980), *Art of the Negro: Native Forms*, 1950-51. Oil on Canvas, panel ⅙, 11 ft. x 11 ft. Clark Atlanta University Art Museum, University Commission, 1952.012; **44**: Courtesy of the Marching "100" Collection,

Meek-Eaton Black Archives & Museum, Florida A&M University; **45**: Collection of the Smithsonian National Museum of African American History and Culture, Gift from Anthony Foster in memory of William P. Foster, 2019.94.1.1; **46**: Permanent Collection, University Museum at Texas Southern; **47**: Permanent Collection, University Museum at Texas Southern, acquisition made possible with funds from the Teiger Foundation; **48**: Tuskegee University Archives, Tuskegee, Alabama; **49**: Tuskegee University Archives, Tuskegee, Alabama; **50**: Margaret Walker Center, Jackson State University; **51**: Margaret Walker Center, Jackson State University; **52**: Collection of the Smithsonian National Museum of African American History and Culture, © 2025 Mora-Catlett Family/ Licensed by VAGA at Artists Rights Society (ARS), NY, 2008.14; **53**: Margaret Walker Center, Jackson State University; **54**: Atlanta University Photographs Collection, Atlanta University Center Robert W. Woodruff Library; **56**: Courtesy of the History of FAMU/School of Nursing Collection, Meek-Eaton Black Archives & Museum, Florida A&M University; **58**: © Kevin Coles; **59**: Tuskegee University, Tuskegee, Alabama; **60**: Jackson State University/Getty Images; **61**: Tuskegee University Archives, Tuskegee, Alabama; **62**: Tuskegee University Archives, Tuskegee, Alabama; **63**: Atlanta University Photographs Collection, Atlanta University Center Robert W. Woodruff Library; **64**: Tuskegee University Archives, Tuskegee, Alabama; **65**: Tuskegee University Archives, Tuskegee, Alabama; **66**: Jackson State University/ Getty Images; **67**: Jackson State University/ Getty Images; **68**: Courtesy of Gloria Batiste-Roberts; **69**: Collection of the Smithsonian National Museum of African American History and Culture, Gift of Texas Southern University; **70**: Courtesy of the Lola Hampton-Frank Pinder Center for Agroecoloogy, Meek-Eaton Black Archives & Museum, Florida A&M University; **71**: © Wilkine Brutus; **73**: Tuskegee University Archives, Tuskegee, Alabama; **74**: Permanent Collection, University Museum at Texas Southern; **77**: Permanent Collection, University Museum at Texas Southern; **78**: Courtesy of Florida Memory; **79**: Student Nonviolent Coordinating Committee Vertical File, Atlanta University Center Robert W. Woodruff Library; **80-81**: Romare Bearden (1914–1980), *Atlanta Mural*, 1976, Collage/ maquette, 7.75 x 34.5 in. Clark Atlanta University Art Museum, Gift of the Artist, 1980.001. © 2025 Romare Bearden Foundation / Licensed by VAGA at Artists Rights Society (ARS), NY; **82**: Tuskegee University Archives, Tuskegee, Alabama; **83**: Courtesy of Chester Higgins Jr.; **84-85**: Permanent Collection, University Museum at Texas Southern; **86-87**: Margaret Walker Center, Jackson State University; **88**: State Archives of Florida; **89**: State Archives of Florida; **90**: Robert King/Getty Images; **91**: Houston Chronicle/Hearst Newspapers/ Getty Images; **92**: Roy DeCarava (1919–2009), *Pickets*, 1946, Seriograph, 12 in. x 9.5 in. Clark Atlanta University Art Museum, Third Atlanta University Purchase Award, Prints, 1946.011; **93**: Shelia Pree Bright (b. 1967). *Young Americans Series: Tarrynn Deavens, age 18, African American*, 2007, Chromogenic print, 39.25 x 29.25. Clark Atlanta University Art Museum, Henry and Judith Acquisition Fund, 2009.005; **Back cover**: Malcolm Heimdall, Heimdall Images, LLC

Frontispiece **Walter T. Bailey instructing students with architectural drawing exhibits**, 1906, Frances Benjamin Johnston (detail) Page 4: *The Boss*, 1932, P. H. Polk (detail)